Thank you God for our day indoors

Eira Reeves

For Charlotte, my goddaughter

Judson Press ® **Valley Forge**

What a gray day! Rain was splashing into puddles outside. Mark and Katie had to play indoors.

What do you like to play indoors?

"Let's be explorers," said Mark. So they sailed off to find new lands.

How do you like to dress up?

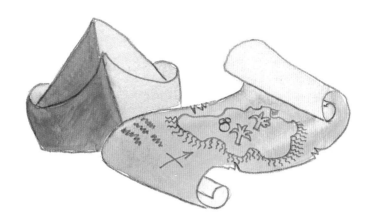

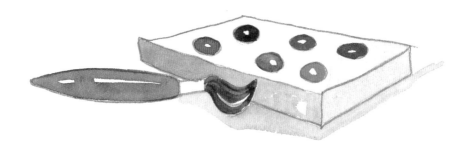

"I'm going to draw a ship for Grandpa," said Katie. "He likes my pictures."

Why don't you draw a picture for someone you know?

"Mommy, I'm bored," said Mark. "What are you making?"
"You can help cut out these cookies," said Mommy.

How many shapes can you see?

After lunch, Katie asked, "Can we watch TV?"
"Good idea. I have a letter to write," said Mommy.

Which program do you like?

"Mommy, Mommy! They're growing seeds on TV. Can we try?" asked Mark. "Yes. We can plant some now," said Mommy.

Have you tried to grow any seeds?

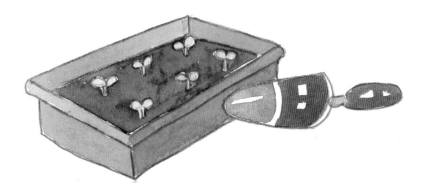

Knock! Knock!
"Who's there?" asked Katie, running to the door.
"It's Susie and Lucy and Richard. We've come to play."

What colors are the raincoats and boots?

"Look! I've got a new cut-out book," said Susie.
"Great! I'll get the scissors," said Mark.

Can you see what they are making?

"I'll tell you a story about the animals in the zoo," said Mommy.
"Great! I'll be a lion," said Mark.
"I'm a kangaroo!" said Katie.

What animal can you pretend to be?

"Would you like a drink?" asked Mommy.
"Yes, please," they all shouted.
"I helped to make the cookies," said
Mark proudly.

Which are your favorite cookies?

Then it was time for Richard, Susie, and Lucy to go.
"Bye! See you tomorrow," said Mark and Katie.

What are your friends' names?

At bedtime Mark and Katie talked to
God and said, "Thank you, God, for our
day indoors."

What did you do today? Tell God about it.

© Eira Reeves 1988   First published 1988
All rights reserved.
Published in the U.S.A. by Judson Press, P.O. Box 851, Valley Forge, PA 19482-0851
ISBN 0-8170-1137-4 U.S.A.
Worldwide co-edition organized and produced by Angus Hudson Ltd., London.
Printed in England by Purnell Book Production Limited